SOUNDS LIKE READING™

BOOK THREE

The Nice Mice in the Rice

A LONG VOWEL SOUNDS BOOK

Brian P. Cleary

illustrations by
Jason Miskimins

Consultant:
Alice M. Maday

Ph.D. in Early Childhood Education with a Focus in Literacy
Assistant Professor, Retired
Department of Curriculum and Instruction
University of Minnesota

M Millbrook Press/Minneapolis

to Sister Editha, my second-grade teacher
in Richfield, Minnesota
—B.P.C.

Millbrook Press
A division of Lerner Publishing Group, Inc.
241 First Avenue North
Minneapolis, MN 55401 U.S.A.

Website address: www.lernerbooks.com

Library of Congress Cataloging-in-Publication Data

Cleary, Brian P., 1959–
    The nice mice in the rice : a long vowel sounds book / by Brian P. Cleary ;
illustrations by Jason Miskimins ; consultant: Alice M. Maday.
        p.   cm. — (Sounds like reading)
    ISBN 978–0–8225–7628–0 (lib. bdg. : alk. paper)
    1. English language—Vowels—Juvenile literature. 2. English language—
Phonetics—Juvenile literature. 3. Reading—Phonetic method—Juvenile
literature. I. Miskimins, Jason, ill. II. Maday, Alice M. III. Title.
PE1157.C55 2009
428.1'3—dc22   2008012774

Manufactured in the United States of America
1 2 3 4 5 6 – BP – 14 13 12 11 10 09

Dear Parents and Educators,

As a former adult literacy coach and the father of three children, I know that learning to read isn't always easy. That's why I developed **Sounds Like Reading**™—a series that uses a combination of devices to help children learn to read.

This book is the third in the **Sounds Like Reading**™ series. It uses rhyme, repetition, illustration, and phonics to introduce young readers to long vowel sounds.

Starting on page 4, you'll see three rhyming words on each left-hand page. These words are part of the sentence on the facing page. They all feature long vowels. As the book progresses, the sentences become more challenging. These sentences contain a "discovery" word—an extra rhyming word in addition to those that appear on the left. Toward the end of the book, the sentences contain two discovery words. Children will delight in the increased confidence that finding and decoding these words will bring. They'll also enjoy looking for the mouse that appears throughout the book. The mouse asks readers to look for words that sound alike.

The bridge to literacy is one of the most important we will ever cross. It is my hope that the **Sounds Like Reading**™ series will help young readers to hop, gallop, and skip from one side to the other!

Sincerely,

Brian P. Cleary

Look for me to help you find the words that sound alike!

Lee

see

bee

Lee can **see** the **bee**.

toad

load

road

Can you find three words that sound alike?

The **toad** takes his **load** on the **road**.

mole

pole

hole

Can you find three words that sound alike?

8

The **mole** and the **pole**
are in the **hole**.

hose

rose

nose

Can you find three words that sound alike?

10

The **hose rose** to my **nose**.

piles

tiles

miles

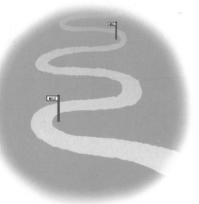

Mile 21

Can you find three words that sound alike?

The **piles** of **tiles** go on for **miles**.

Jake

make

rake

Can you find the word that sounds like Jake, make, and rake?

Jake can **make** a **cake**
with a **rake**.

vase

lace

case

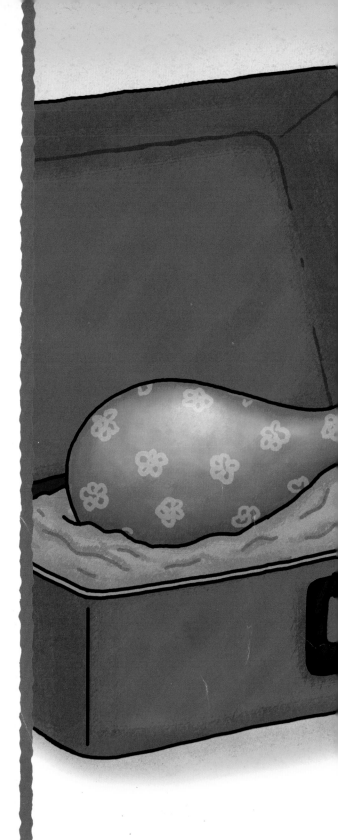

Can you find the word that sounds like vase, lace, and case?

The **ace**, the **vase**, and the **lace** are in the **case**.

nine

dine

vine

Can you find the word that sounds like nine, dine, and vine?

18

A **line** of **nine dine** on the **vine**.

goat

coat

moat

Can you find the word that sounds like goat, coat, and moat?

The **goat** in the **boat** dropped his **coat** in the **moat**.

mice

rice

dice

Can you find the word that sounds like mice, rice, and dice?

The **nice mice** in the **rice** played **dice**.

seat

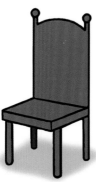

meat

neat

Can you find the word that sounds like seat, meat, and neat?

24

Sit in your **seat**, **eat** your **meat**, and be **neat**.

Jay

hay

bay

Can you find two words that sound like Jay, hay, and bay?

Jay may lay some **hay** by the **bay**.

Gail

nail

pail

Can you find two words that sound like Gail, nail, and pail?

Gail will **fail** to find a **nail** or a **pail** in the **mail.**

ride

wide

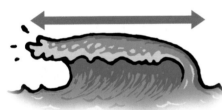

tide

Can you find two words that sound like ride, wide, and tide?

Hide on the **side**, and **ride**
on the **wide tide**.

Brian P. Cleary is the author of the best-selling Words Are CATegorical® series as well as the Math Is CATegorical® and Adventures in Memory™ series. He has also written several picture books and poetry books. In addition to his work as a children's author and humorist, Mr. Cleary has been a tutor in an adult literacy program. He lives in Cleveland, Ohio.

Jason Miskimins grew up in Cincinnati, Ohio, and graduated from the Columbus College of Art & Design in 2003. He currently lives in North Olmsted, Ohio, where he works as an illustrator of books and greeting cards.

Alice M. Maday has a master's degree in early childhood education from Butler University in Indianapolis, Indiana, and a Ph.D. in early childhood education, with a focus in literacy, from the University of Minnesota in Minneapolis. Dr. Maday has taught at the college level as well as in elementary schools and preschools throughout the country. In addition, she has served as an emergent literacy educator for kindergarten and first-grade students in Germany for the U.S. Department of Defense. Her research interests include the kindergarten curriculum, emergent literacy, parent and teacher expectations, and the place of preschool in the reading readiness process.

For even more phonics fun, check out all eight SOUNDS LIKE READING™ titles listed on the back of this book!

And find activities, games, and more at www.brianpcleary.com.